Growing and Caring for Tomatoes
A Tomato Growing Book

By Brian Stephens

via Amazon Createspace
© Brian Stephens 2014
(ISBN: 978-1492144250)

Contents

Introduction

Tomatoes are a true favourite right across the gardening world. The reason is obvious. Following these simple, but important, guidelines, anyone can get a great crop of tasty tomatoes even with limited resources in terms of garden space. They can be grown in pots on a patio, hanging upside down, in a garden plot, a greenhouse or in a strategically placed grow-bag.

Tomatoes come in all shapes, colours and sizes and can be used in salads, as an ingredient in a variety of hot dishes, as a sauce to accompany pasta or just eaten on their own as a tasty fruit. And the left-over green, still to ripen, varieties can make a very tasty pickle or preserve.

Beefsteak tomatoes

Simply put, there is no need to waste a single tomato you have grown; each and every type has a use, and even if they don't make it to full maturity on the vine, there are tips and tricks to bring them on or you can just use them as they are. Once you have tasted a fabulous green tomato chutney you will know what I mean.

The essential ingredients for growing tomatoes are sun, plenty of it, and sufficient regular watering. These are the two key elements, but there are other aspects you need to take care of to ensure you get the most from your plants and do not find yourself feeling fed up and dejected at the end of the growing season. All this will be explained in the following chapters in an order that you should find logical and easy to understand.

The techniques to be described are essentially 'organic' in nature, not because that was a philosophical decision, but because taking a natural approach will cost less and enable a home gardener to utilise the resources readily available, even if there is a little more effort and input required.

That said, the rewards you get from growing and caring for tomatoes properly far outweigh the effort, the tomato really is a very generous plant. Even in differing climates, and some that are not always ideal, for example in the UK you may need to select a plant that matures early, or use a greenhouse. But generally, where there is a will there is a way.

Points of Interest - What is a tomato?

You think you know what a tomato is? I thought I knew what tomatoes were (and that's the plural form – with toes). Then I consulted my dictionaries! Now I'm not sure. Is it a berry, a fruit, a vegetable, a herb, a plant? The odd man out here is without doubt the vegetable – but don't let the United States Supreme Court hear you say that. In their wisdom they ruled it to be just that in 1893 and now stand alone in their definition of a tomato as a vegetable. The rest of the world considers it a red or yellow pulpy edible fruit.

The botanical name for the plant is **Lycopersicon**. How these botanists do so love their Greek. Apparently this can be translated as wolf peach. Marvellous! Most helpful. But things get worse, much worse. The botanists then decided to study this plant's relations and place it in a family tree. Now we're in for a shock. Not only is the tomato related to the potato, an association I'm quite happy with . . . on the plate, but it also shares genes with the nightshade family, which includes, as we all know, Uncle Deadly. No wonder people once thought the tomato poisonous. And they were right. There are categories of wild tomatoes that can be highly so, but even a keen and diligent botanist would have to search hard to find them.

Acknowledgements

Before getting into the nitty gritty of the guide, I would just like to briefly mention that I may have penned this book but the inspiration and knowledge has been passed on by Hubert Francis Stephens, a master gardener with the greenest of green fingers.

He was born and raised in a period that saw him having to survive both the Second World War and a serious accident in a coal pit where he worked for a while as a miner. It was also a time when, living at home as a child, the nearest water source was a good three-quarters of a mile away at the village well. There was no piped water back then, only the biggest bucket that he or his brothers could carry.

Hubert Francis Stephens

He lived with his eight brothers and sisters in a two up, two down cottage in a rural part of the Royal Forest of Dean. For those that don't know, this is deep in Gloucestershire, England. Nestled between the River Severn and the River Wye, the Royal Forest of Dean used to be the hunting ground of kings and formed a significant part of Gloucestershire. In modern times it is the favourite home county of members of the British Royal Family.

Home for a family of ten!

In the nineteen-thirties, keeping a family pig and tending the garden was not a favourite hobby or pastime, but rather a case of ensuring a sustainable lifestyle. To have a bad year in the garden literally meant having no food to put on your plate. Not being able to look after your garden properly was considered sacrilege, you had to be master of your trade back in those days just to survive.

This is probably the reason why his plants always flourished and became potential prize winners. It didn't seem to matter whether it was a flower, a cactus or, of course, his beloved tomatoes.

He may no longer be with us, but his tips and tricks for growing the best tomatoes are now captured for ever in this book which is dedicated to his memory

Seed and Plant Types - Selection

Tomato Types

There are two general types of tomato, determinate or bush tomatoes, and indeterminate or vine tomatoes (also known as cordon tomatoes).

Bush tomatoes grow to determinate size and tend to produce all their fruit over a relatively short period.

Vine or cordon tomatoes grow to an indeterminate size, that can be controlled by pruning, and develop trusses as they grow from the bottom to the top of the plant. A truss is an individual cluster of blossom with its own stalk. The lowest truss (nearest the root) develops and produces its fruit first, followed in turn by the second lowest truss and so on. Consequently, vine tomatoes produce their fruit over an extended period of time as the plant grows, the trusses develop and the blossom turns into fruit.

You should select bush or vine tomatoes depending on your requirements and the space you have available for your tomato plants.

Tomatoes from the Vine

11

Clearly the types of tomatoes you can grow will depend on the location and space you have to grow them. But there are some other considerations:

- *flavour*, if you are looking for a tastier variety then you should probably be thinking of selecting one of the Heirloom varieties. These have been kept going, not by the market gardeners and supermarket suppliers, but rather by the tomato-growing enthusiasts who care less about transport-toughness and shelf-life than they do about getting the tastiest tomatoes.

With respect to what is the tastiest tomato variety it was reported by 'Which Magazine', a UK consumer advice publication, that one of the tastiest of tomatoes, identified through consumer trials, is the Sioux tomato; this is of American origin and one of the Heirloom varieties.

Sioux Tomatoes

The second tastiest tomatoes were listed as being the 'Orkado' tomatoes and, while we are at it, the worst and most bland-tasting tomato was identified as, can you bear it, the 'Alicante' - a firm favourite with many mass retailers.

- *high yielding,* clearly, if you want a decent crop of tomatoes then you should select a high-yielding variety. Refer to the information on the packet or plant label or seek the advice of assistants in your local area for suggestions. Not every high yielding option will thrive in your specific geographic location so a little bit of professional advice will point you in the right direction.

- *disease resistance,* make sure that they have a natural resistance to fusarium wilt and verticillium; these are two of the most common tomato diseases that tomatoes can get from the ground. This information is usually displayed on seed packets or plant labels.

- *open pollinating or hybrid,* this relates to whether you have ambitions to sow your own seeds. Never try and cultivate seeds that have been recovered from the 'hybrid' varieties of tomatoes. These have been specially developed for specific characteristics and cannot simply be used to grow tomatoes in a domestic environment. They just will not grow into a plant due to the fact the seed produced by hybrids is sterile.

That said, you are probably wondering which tomatoes can be used to harvest your own seed for cultivating and the answer is pretty much any of the non-hybrid variety. Some are easier than others and the most popular seeds cultivated by gardeners are the heirloom varieties for the reasons stated earlier.

- *time to ripening,* this needs to be considered with respect to the climate of your location. If your growing season is short then you need to be aware whether in the time available you will actually achieve a crop of ripe tomatoes. Some regions stay sunny for longer and the use of a greenhouse can extend your season. Typically it is the larger varieties of tomatoes that take the longest to ripen, so choosing smaller varieties should ensure you get some ripe ones. More on ripening later.

Dwarf tomatoes are small and compact

Tomato Size

Tomatoes grow in different sizes. Generally you can select from Cherry, Standard, Plum or Beefsteak tomatoes, with Cherry being the smallest fruit that tends to come in bite-sized tomatoes and Beefsteak the largest which can be sliced for a salad or burger.

It is the size of the tomatoes that primarily dictates how long they take to mature; cherry tomatoes generally slot into the early season variety, mid size such as plum tomatoes tend to go in the mid season grouping and larger tomatoes like beefsteak fit in the late season group. It's a good idea to have plants from the different varieties to ensure you have tomatoes maturing throughout the whole season.

- early season varieties, no more than 60 days to ripen

- mid season varieties, no more than 75 days to ripen

- late season varieties, no more than 90 days to ripen

Tomato Uses

Consider how you want to use your tomatoes before selecting your seeds or plants. Typically the cherry tomatoes are great for salads and eating straight from the plant, standard tomatoes are general purpose and can be used both for salads and cooking, plum tomatoes are a good cooking choice and beefsteak are again great for slicing into a burger or for a salad but can also be used for cooking.

Which tomatoes grow best where?

With around 7500 different tomato varieties to choose from, finding the tomato that suits you and the region you live in can be a little bit like finding a needle in a haystack.

A way to easily narrow down the choice and still stand a chance of finding one that will thrive in your location is to see what the local garden centre or store are stocking. That should at least help you find a tomato variety that will grow in your region.

For the United States, you might be interested in the following list of tomatoes that will grow pretty much anywhere, from North Central down to the Gulf Coast and both to the east and to the west

- Beefsteak

- Brandy Wine

- Early Girl

- Cherokee Purple

- Super Sweet 100

- Black Cherry

- Roma

- Amish Paste

- Saint Marzano

This list gives you a choice of hybrids or heirlooms, cooking tomatoes to salad tomatoes and a pretty sure-fired chance that they will all cope with the climate in your region. In other words they are all safe bets for a good crop of tomatoes across a range of shapes and sizes that should suit most requirements.

There will of course be specific varieties that may be even more suitable for your specific location, so the other indicators and ways of establishing which tomatoes grow best, and where, still stand and may just lead you to exactly what you are looking for.

Points of Interest - Where on earth do tomatoes come from?

In its native habitat, the tomato plant was a perennial: one that lasted from one year to the next, and fruited regularly. But this habitat needed to be tropical not temperate. Nowadays the tomato is routinely treated and cultivated as an annual – because most of the world's population live in non-tropical climes.

History books suggest that South America is the home of the tomato, and what can't be challenged is the fact that the name was recorded by Spanish invaders there from the native Nahuatl 'tomatl' which morphed into tomate and then became anglicised as tomato.

The Aztecs of Central America are known to have used tomatoes, and some say the plant's origins are to be found in Peru. Historians, however, agree that the tomato was brought to Europe four hundred or so years ago . . . and salads have never been the same since. 1544 is the earliest reference found for a European-grown tomato, the Italian botanist Mattioli calling it the pomo d'oro which translates as golden apple.

Like most newcomers, tomatoes were by no means instantly welcomed when they first docked in Europe. Indeed in Britain the natives were extremely suspicious of the plant and suspected a devious plot to undermine public health. The tomato was branded by many as poisonous. Who knows why? Perhaps the wild and toxic cousin of our now much loved fruit had been consumed unwisely by an influential traveller and the whole family of tomatoes had been convicted on the spot. No matter, in time the tomato was adopted throughout Europe and the Americas until today it is a favoured ingredient in most great cooks' armoury.

Tomato Planting Schedule

The easiest way to describe the start of any tomato planting schedule anywhere in the world is to state that you cannot afford your plants to be exposed to any sort of frost. In the UK, for example, it would be taking a serious risk to have your plants in the ground before May has arrived unless of course you have a heated greenhouse or are able to protect the early plants in some other way from a sudden frost.

Propagating from seed should begin between four and six weeks prior to the anticipated date when the actual plants need to be going into their final planting location. The ideal germination temperature for tomato seeds is around 16C (61F).

Considering how long the tomato plants take to mature, based on the three groups mentioned earlier, you should allow the following time-frames:

- early season varieties need 60 days

- mid season varieties need 75 days

- late season varieties need 90 days

Basically what you have to ensure is that any plants you put in, where you want to achieve a fully ripened condition, need sufficient time to ripen before the frosts and inclement weather of the following autumn arrive.

Taking into account when you are likely to see the last frost of the previous winter, you can establish the earliest time you can get your plants into their final planting position.

To further extend the season, work backwards from when you are likely to see the first frost of the autumn. Then, dependent on the variety you have chosen, you can determine the latest time for getting plants into their final position. If for example you select an early season variety you will need to have the plants in place at least 60 days before the first frost of the autumn, because then they will still potentially have time to ripen.

Don't forget that sometimes you may not require a fully ripened tomato. Some people deliberately grow tomatoes that they know may not ripen because they want to use them for preserves such as green tomato chutney, a delicious way to use up excess tomatoes for very little effort.

Growing Tomatoes from Seed

You can if you like extract the seeds from your own tomatoes, as demonstrated in the video link I have provided. Essentially once you have the seeds from tomatoes they are no different to any other garden seed and the process of propagation is much the same as for any other plant.

(http://myhomegrowntomatoes.com/growing-tomato-seed/)

Top Tip - You cannot grow plants with seeds taken from Hybrid tomatoes as mentioned earlier. These hybrids have been developed for specific characteristics and the seed cannot be used to grow tomatoes in a domestic environment because they are sterile.

Preparations: -

Use ripe, reasonably fresh seed that has been stored in a cool dry place

Use proper seed compost for best results; loam-based seed compost is generally the best

Maintain a good level of cleanliness both of the compost (keep it in sealed bags) and of the seed trays

Fill the seed trays to about 1/2 an inch (12mm) below their top rim by pressing in your seed compost, levelling it off and firming it down by hand

Mark the tray so you that know what you have planted

Moisten the compost before starting to sow so that it is exactly that: moist - which means neither dry nor waterlogged.

Push the seeds into the compost to a depth equal to their diameter or thereabouts, tweezers might help with this process.

Don't sow everything at once. Stagger over a week or two to give your plants different stages of development and consequently a longer growing period overall.

Make sure the seed is lightly covered, and then water in with a fine mist of water from a sprayer.

That is pretty much it; you can help the seeds along by covering with a sheet of white paper and a piece of glass or slipping the seed tray into a polythene bag to help retain moisture. The paper stops the condensation going straight into the seed compost.

After two to three weeks the seedlings should be large enough to handle without damage and should then be transplanted, using tweezers or a thin plastic or wooden strip with a V notched out to prise out the root ball. Try not to handle the stem; hold the plant by the first leaf.

Use a dibber to make a small hole in the compost and put two to three seedlings in a 3" pot ready to grow on. Leave them now to grow until they are large enough for planting in the ground or some kind of container.

Vine tomatoes usually do well for the final stage if they are planted two or three to a 40L grow bag or one per 12" pot. Other than that, of course, you can prepare the soil and plant your tomatoes in the ground. Raised beds are an excellent option, but for short summer regions they should probably be in a greenhouse.

Remember before final planting to check the plants over and discard any that are weak, stunted, distorted or where the leaves are pale or mottled. These are the ones most susceptible to disease and are liable to fail at the final stage.

Top Tip just a reminder that the ideal germination temperature for tomatoes is 16C (61F).

Planting your Tomatoes

Location

Selecting a location for planting tomatoes comes down to considering two aspects: first, what the tomato plant needs to flourish and secondly the practicalities of looking after them.

So focussing on the first aspect, it is common knowledge that tomatoes need sunshine, sunshine in abundance, and that means a minimum of six hours a day. They wouldn't suffer and would probably enjoy up to ten hours a day, so that is your first consideration and what it means is you need to identify a position that gets sun most of the day. By providing this amount of exposure to the sunshine you will be pretty much ensuring that your tomatoes will ripen readily and that you will not be left with a whole harvest of green tomatoes.

Tomato plants are not that robust; this is the reason you have to tie them up with soft string or find some other means that will not damage them. It follows then that if they are being battered by wind, or are exposed to odd bouts of severe weather, then they are likely to become damaged and perhaps you could lose a few trusses or maybe even a whole plant. So do them a favour and find a sheltered spot. Being close to a wall or fence will go a long way towards protecting the plants, providing you keep them on the sunny side of course.

For the second aspect, caring for tomatoes, this primarily refers to watering; when watering the practicalities are that ideally they need to be watered little and often. So unless you have some sort of automatic watering system plumbed in you need to be physically delivering water to your plants on a regular basis. So planting near a source of water is the best solution.

Finally, tomatoes need to be inspected regularly for signs of disease or pests. Basically you will need easy access to the plants so that you can inspect, treat and prune them as required without walking on the soil between them.

If you don't have the facilities to provide these ideal conditions, it's not the end of the world. You just need to work with what you've got. This will mean careful plant selection so that you can deal with the conditions the plants have to grow under. For example, choose an early-maturing variety if you have limited sunshine. Perhaps grow cherry tomato varieties if you are tight on space, or use containers on a patio if your garden is very small or you don't actually have one. Where there is a will there is a way and when you produce your first fruit you will be glad you persevered.

Soil Preparation

For best results tomatoes need a well-drained and loamy soil with a pH of between six and seven ideally (but they can cope with 5.5 to 9.5). They also need a good supply of nitrogen, so prepare your soil by forking in a good mix of nitrogen-rich compost and well-rotted manure. If you want to be super efficient you can dig a trench about 18" deep and put in a layer of newspaper at the bottom; this will help retain moisture.

Making your own compost is environmentally friendly, very easy and will save you money. So instead of using compost bought from a garden centre or garden supply store, why not, if you can, set up a little corner of your plot for recycling your kitchen waste and garden cuttings. Tomatoes need loose soil which has plenty of nutrients in order to form a decent root system. By making a compost pile in your garden you can ensure that you have the main ingredient you need for proper soil preparation.

Mix topsoil with compost and a well-rotted manure mix (if you can get it) to fill the trench. After planting you can add a further mulch to the top of the soil to help further with moisture retention and to keep weeds under control. Remember tomatoes like warm damp feet so don't be too quick with the surface mulch as this will tend to prevent the soil warming, especially early in the growing season.

Acclimatise the Tomato Plants

Try not to shock your plants by planting them straight from the greenhouse or indoors overnight. Introduce them to the great outdoors a little bit at a time. Put them out during the day in a shady spot and bring them back in at night for about ten to fourteen days. This will make them more hardy and likely to survive, as long of course as they are not exposed to frost as it will only take one frost exposure to kill them.

The Planting

When the plants have been acclimatised you can either plant them in pots, grow-bags or soil prepared as described above. The plants will need to be spaced approximately 18" (450mm) apart if being planted in soil and should be planted deep enough for the soil to be up to the first leaves of the plant.

Top tip – plant pots should be no smaller than 12 inches (300mm) diameter for final planting, leaving about 1/2 an inch (12mm) of space below the rim for adding fresh compost as the plant grows and the original compost shrinks in size. Also if you use a 40L grow-bag never put in more than three plants; if you have room it's even better to keep it to two plants per grow-bag.

It is fair to say that a lot of the problems associated with growing tomatoes are the consequences of using diseased soil that has reached this condition as a result of many years of continual use. So using containers can solve this problem. You use fresh compost in your containers (or grow-bags) so the contamination problem is no longer an issue, provided you disinfect any containers that you are re-using before planting.

That said, my favourite way to grow tomatoes is in a raised bed. Growing tomatoes in a raised bed is a great way to ensure that you can grow healthy tomato plants in a controlled area and in reasonable quantities. There are lots of ways to build a raised bed for tomatoes and vegetables. Use this link to see a video that describes many of most common methods with detailed instructions for how to build a raised bed using a basic timber structure.

(http://myhomegrowntomatoes.com/build-raised-bed-tomatoes/)

You should also consider what materials you already have available. For example, as I have a reasonable amount of timber on my land, I simply cut down a few appropriately sized logs i.e. around 6″ (150mm) diameter and cut them to the required length. The recommended size when building a raised bed is 4'(1.2m) by 2'(0.6m) This will ensure that you can easily access the entire area of the raised bed without having to stand on the soil. So weeding, pest control and general maintenance can easily be carried out from the edges of the raised bed. It also makes it easier to stake your individual plants, which should be spaced at least 18″ (450mm) apart, to ensure they have sufficient light and nutrients. Six plants will fit reasonably comfortably in a raised bed of this size.

By using materials that are already available you can save on the cost of purchasing timber from the local garden centre or DIY outlet. So it is always worth looking to see what you have and if there is something suitable then why not use it? A raised bed made of wood does not have to be an exact science, and as long as it is reasonably substantial and can take the weather for a few years it will be fine.

If after a period of use you think it might be a good idea to change the soil - worries of contamination and disease - then it will not be too arduous a task to dig out the soil and start again from scratch.

Simple Raised Beds

Growing Tomatoes in a Greenhouse

One of the main reasons for using a greenhouse when growing tomatoes is because of the climate you live in. If you cannot guarantee warm sunny weather for your tomatoes then you will need to consider using a greenhouse. This will help you control the climate for the tomato plants and give them a better chance of producing lots of edible fruit.

There are a couple of ways for approaching tomato growing in a greenhouse: you can either dig and prepare the soil of the greenhouse ready to accept the tomato plants or you can grow the plants in a container such as a plant pot or grow-bag.

If you go for pots then you should sterilise them before use. To do this you can use a dilute solution of a suitable disinfectant, something like Jeyes fluid is perfect for this task.

While we are on this subject, you really should wipe down the inside of your greenhouse with disinfectant as well to ensure any residual contaminants that could also cause disease are removed from the glass.

One of the reasons I am suggesting using large pots or grow-bags for growing tomato plants is because the soil in the greenhouse is going to need to be dug out and replaced every two or three years anyway to ensure that you get rid of any build up of disease, and also because the soil will be pretty much spent in terms of nutrients.

Space is limited in a greenhouse so the best option for plant varieties is to use the indeterminate variety of tomato plant i.e. a vine plant. You can prune the plant to the required size, leaving about four to six trusses on the main stem, which is about 6' to 7' in height, greenhouse size allowing. This will give you lots of fruit over an extended period. You will have to pinch out the main stem when you have enough trusses to stop further growth.

As an aside, using the bush variety is less convenient for greenhouses because they, as the name suggests, form a determinant size of bush without pruning which is probably a little too limiting for the average greenhouse. The fruit also has a tendency to all come at once. Using vine tomatoes on the other hand means you can optimise your use of the available space through pruning.

Top Tip - gently shake the plants when they are in flower to help pollination. I emphasize gently, and remember, there is no breeze inside a greenhouse, so this is simply to aid a process that would normally happen naturally outside with a little bit of breeze going on and the friendly assistance of passing bees.

No that's not a pollination feature!

Irrespective of the growing method you choose, you should start to feed the tomatoes at the first sign of fruit and for the duration of the growing period. Twice a week is a good rule of thumb. But simply following the instructions for the feed you chose is probably better. As you are in a greenhouse, regular and consistent watering is also important and two to three times a day with water that has been allowed to warm in the greenhouse is recommended.

You also need to take care not to let the greenhouse get too hot and or humid. If it is really sunny for a period you can paint the glass with a whitewash to reflect the sun away and you can open the roof light or door to let some of the heat out but don't forget to shut them again at night when it is cooler.

As the end of the season nears, a way of helping the last remaining fruit ripen is to hang a couple of bananas in the apex of the greenhouse.

Supporting Tomato Plants

There are various ways of supporting tomato plants: you can use a simple stake pushed in next to the plant, taking care not to damage the roots; you can use a form of tomato or plant cage, or you can create a structure yourself using strong stakes and garden string, a little like a series of washing lines.

Use a soft garden string to tie off the plants; they damage easily so you cannot tie too tightly or use ties that will cause damage such as garden wire. Select a spot on the plant that will support the trusses, ideally under a leaf node. You will need to do this as the weight of the fruit, when it comes, could easily snap an unsupported stem or at least bend it down to the ground where the fruit can spoil, or worse, become contaminated.

Determinate type plants may not need staking; you can keep an eye on the plants to see what they are doing. It doesn't hurt of course to support them if you think the fruit is going to hang down to the ground or if you think things are a little overcrowded. A plant cage will hold the fruit up and you can arrange the plant for better air circulation. This is a bit of a judgment call really which you need to decide on yourself.

As I tend to grow vine tomatoes my preferred option is to use a strong stake pushed into the soil next to each plant that is tall enough to support around six trusses. Then as the plant grows I just tie the trusses to the stake using the preferred soft garden string which much reduces the chance of damaging the plant.

A slightly different approach to supporting tomato plants is the upside down planting or topsy-turvy system. This is where you hang a plant upside down from a stand or rafter. Vine tomatoes are more suited to this approach as they hang down vertically and with a little bit of clever tomato pruning can be constrained into very small spaces.

It's possible to make your own upside down planter using a disused plastic bucket if you have a little time to spare. Search on www.youtube.com for detailed instructions if you are not sure how to go about it.

Points of Interest - Vital statistics about the tomato

I grow my tomatoes in small quantities. Indeed I can usually count the number of plants I put into my raised beds on one hand. But statisticians have other ideas – they think big . . . and heavy.

As I write this I'm consulting a table of statistics that quotes worldwide production by country, and talks of metric tons. Now to me that sure is a lot of tomatoes. A kilo or a pound at a time I can manage, at a push. But a metric ton, now that's really something. And the revelation: we have all shrugged off our worries about the tomato being dangerous to eat – over forty million metric tons are now processed most years, and these figures exclude home and locally grown beauties: the type I prefer to indulge in. I suspect the tomato is here to stay.

A figure I can more readily understand concerns 'per-capita' consumption in the United States. This suggests that if you take all the mouths available there, large and small, then allocate to each an equal ration of tomatoes, you'll be popping in nearly twenty pounds of tomatoes (over 9 kilos) a year. And this appetite is growing fast, as the statistics reveal.

Tomato Pruning

Determinate-type tomato plants typically do not require pruning, although as previously mentioned, a little thinning out to promote good air circulation won't do any harm.

Indeterminate tomato plants, however, do require pruning. Firstly, to prevent contamination from the soil, it is a good idea to prune off all the suckers below the first truss. Then you need to decide how many vines you want to grow; this could range between one to three, but it is fair to say that most people would probably settle for two.

You can of course just have a single vine by removing all suckers. Or, by allowing a stem to grow just above the first fruit truss, you can get a second vine, and for a third stem allow the next one up to remain and develop into a vine.

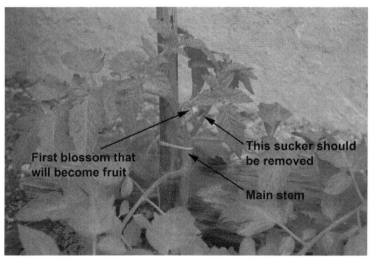

This sucker should be removed

First blossom that will become fruit

Main stem

Another reason for pruning is to control the number of trusses per vine you want. Normally you would be looking for between four to six trusses on a vine dependent on the length of your growing season. The longer the season the more trusses you can get to the ripening stage. It also depends on whether you are growing in a greenhouse or outside; using a greenhouse helps prolong your season.

Pruning can also be used to help the ripening process; removing some of the growth with no blossom will help divert energy to the fruit, and removing blossoms that are not going to make it into ripened fruit will do the same thing. This type of pruning is done from around mid season towards the end of the season, when you are trying to bring the crops home. Don't prune too much though; there is a balance between maintaining a healthy plant, good air circulation and re-directing the plants energy to the right places.

Visit How to Prune Tomatoes for a video demonstration of the procedure.

(myhomegrowntomatoes.com/stringing-suckering-tomato-plants)

Tomato Watering

Tomatoes do need a lot of water but they should, as previously stated, not be waterlogged or over-watered. The ideal situation is a consistently moist condition achieved through a regular and consistent watering schedule, either through a disciplined manual routine, or by using an automatic watering system.

As tomatoes reach the ripening stage you can actually back off on the watering a little to ensure you have a nice firm but juicy fruit. Again this is a bit of a judgment call which you may need to determine through experimentation. The plants should not be struggling for water but what you can use as a rule of thumb is to allow the surface of the soil to dry out as long as you are sure you still have sufficient moisture below the immediate surface.

In the interest of maintaining warm moist feet it is a good idea, as part of your watering programme, to allow the water to warm to air temperature before applying. This is not as difficult as it sounds; you just fill your cans with water, allow them to sit overnight, and then refill after watering for the next day. This prevents any shocking or cooling of the plant roots.

Many of the problems people encounter with their tomato crops arise from irregular watering and or extremes of temperature. These include blossom end rot, split skins, flower shedding and ripening problems. but there are more.

People these days can lead very hectic lifestyles and are constantly under time pressure to get everything done, so taking care of the garden can sometimes drop down the list of priorities. For those people I would say that considering an automatic garden watering system of some sort is a good way of making sure that you address at least one of the tomato care factors that are important for ensuring a full and healthy crop.

There are a number of options available that vary in both price and efficiency to suit your budget and the level of assistance you need. These can range from a simple roll mat that sits under your plant pots to a full blown Micro Water Irrigation System.

If you do decide on a fully automatic system don't forget that you will still need to check your plants for other problems, such as pests or disease. One of the benefits of a daily watering routine that you do yourself is that you visit and see your plants regularly and can spot problems before it is too late.

One final point on watering tomatoes is with respect to the taste. Understanding what makes the tastiest tomatoes might help a little. The watering programme to a relatively significant extent can affect taste i.e. if you over-water then there is a risk you will make your tomatoes watery and a little bland.

What it comes down to is getting the level of watering right so that you get a concentrated flavour as a result. Over-water and potentially you end up with watery, bland tomatoes. Maintain your watering program so that the soil is just moist, and there is a good chance that you will get the tasty tomatoes you are looking for. As the fruit reaches the final ripening stage you can consider backing off on the watering programme a little so that you err on the side of a drier soil, but not completely dry.

This is of course a little subjective and down to trial and error with your chosen tomato varieties. The main reason for raising the point is that if you are finding varieties recommended for their taste are still bland, you may need to consider your watering regime.

Tomato Feeding

If you have prepared your soil with nitrogen-rich compost and well-rotted manure mix then you will be well on the way to ensuring that your plants will get all the nutrients they need.

Other ways of feeding your plants include the use of nitrogen-rich mulch or by using a feed supplement. How often you apply the supplement depends very much on the type selected, many people follow the twice a week rule mentioned earlier. But what I would suggest is that you use a formulated tomato feed and follow the instructions supplied with the product.

Plants in containers or grow-bags will need a regular supplement, but for plants that have been put into the ground it is less critical. Also bear in mind that you can overfeed your plants and that this is as detrimental as not providing enough feed, so the obvious way around this is to stick to the instructions and not to get too feed happy.

Pest Control

Check your tomato plants regularly for any signs of pest infestation. Typical pest attacks can come from whitefly or aphids, the most common, but there are others. See below for the full list of common pests. Make sure you lift the leaves to look underneath as this is where the pesky little creatures tend to hide.

If you find you have a problem then there are various ways of dealing with them, but it is important you take immediate action as the problem will quickly escalate.

Some of the most common tomato pests are: -

- aphids

- whitefly

- spider mites

- leafhoppers

- flea beetles

- tomato hornworm

- earwigs

The above isn't by any means the full list of pests, but there are common ways to rid yourself of all pests. For instance, when they are still eggs and if you are not too squeamish, you can simply wipe them off by pinching the leaves gently between your fingers and thumb and using your thumb to squash the eggs and wipe them off the leaf at the same time. A bit messy but effective.

Larger bugs like caterpillars can be picked off and dropped into a jam jar with some appropriate cocktail that will see them off.

An effective way of dealing with whitefly is to mix a fluid of one part liquid soap and four parts water in a spray bottle and dowse the whole plant with the mix.

Earwigs, believe it or not, like a beer. So if you are having trouble with these little fellas, it's time to throw a party. A good technique is to bury a container half filled with beer in the ground beneath your tomato plants. You can leave it sticking out of the ground a little and when the earwigs turn up they head for a beer bath. Shame they only have little legs and can't swim, but then they were the ones that decided your prized tomato plants were a prime target, so no mercy I am afraid.

There is also the option of encouraging tomato friendly bugs that feed on the unfriendly bugs; a good example is a ladybug (ladybird as it is known in the UK). The normal technique is to put plants which attract the good bugs interspersed or close to your tomato plants. For a full list of friendly bugs and the plants that attract them search for the 'Natural Enemies Handbook' or visit Plants That Attract Beneficial Insects as an online resource.

(www.farmerfred.com/plants_that_attract_benefi.html)

You also have the option of using chemical pesticides, of course, but I have to be honest that there are so many different types that I think what most people need is a pest control book or bible. This one is an affordable option for anyone that wants a guide to dealing with all manner of pests.

(www.amazon.com/dp/0520221079)

Points of Interest - Tomatoes are not just for eating

When Cortes or Columbus first shipped the tomato back from the Americas (no customs' records exist!) many regarded the tomato as an object of beauty rather than an item for the cook to cherish. And even today the tomato can be employed to good effect outside the kitchen.

And teenagers might find one reference I've dug up most useful. Apparently it's good at getting rid of blockheads. I found this puzzling for a while – until I realised a typo had crept in. Now blackheads are indeed a curse worth eradicating and a slice of tomato contains both vitamin C and a mild acid that clears pores and dead skin. For those with less than perfect complexions therefore, an application of finely sliced tomatoes applied to the face when lying down might work wonders in short sessions. However, I suggest keeping this book to hand in case of intruders otherwise your reputation might take a dive.

Tomato Problems

There is a range of tomato problems that you could encounter, but as a rule of thumb if you maintain a regular and consistent watering programme, protect your plants from extremes of temperature and prevent the plant from contacting the soil through correct pruning and support then you will almost certainly avoid most of, if not all, the causes of tomato problems.

Tomato blossom end rot is a common tomato disease where the lower half or blossom end becomes brown and dry.

There are a number of potential causes for this including the wrong soil type, too much nitrogen and extremes of either wet or dry weather.

Tomatoes don't really like limey or sandy soil so if the ground you are using has this constituency you are either going to have to use containers or be extra vigilant when preparing the soil. A good idea for the latter is to dig a trench, line the bottom with newspaper and then fill it back in with a good well-rotted compost and soil mix, potentially getting soil from another source if yours really is very sandy or full of lime.

If you think that perhaps you have overfed the plants with nitrogen then just stop feeding for a while and if you have put down a high nitrogen mulch, like coffee grounds, you can scrape it back off and try to eradicate the source.

A scenario called variable soil moisture has also been known to cause this condition, which is why it is a good idea to perform consistent and regular watering of the plants to establish a situation where the soil is neither saturated nor ever dries out. This point cannot be stressed enough, as you are probably beginning to realise.

With a little extra attention to your preparation and ongoing care it is relatively easy to avoid blossom end rot.

Many of the most common tomato problems actually originate from just two causes: -

- the famous erratic watering

- erratic temperatures

These two causes are often responsible for a whole range of problems with tomatoes: -

- flower shedding

- blossom end rot, as previously discussed

- immature fruit fall

- split skins

- sun scald

- blotchy ripening

- tomatoes not ripening

Of course temperature extremes is the most difficult of the two causes to manage as you are very much at the mercy of mother nature and what she throws at you. Certainly where we are in the South of France, it is not unusual to see temperatures of up to 37C (100F) during the summer on occasion which will actually halt the ripening process.

If you have a greenhouse then you do have options for whitening the glass or opening doors and windows when the temperature is very warm. There are automatic window openers available that operate on a temperature basis, to make this easier to manage, and other than that you just have to do things manually.

Ideally you want to keep your temperatures constant and somewhere between 18C (65F) and 21C (70F), the minimum temperature you can live with is about 13C (55F) and the maximum is around 29C (85F).

Out of doors this will be difficult to control, so for cooler climates you may need a greenhouse and for warmer climates you can try temporary shading at the hottest part of the day or you can perhaps position them so that they don't get full sun at the hottest part of the day, a little tricky because you still need sufficient sun to ripen the tomatoes i.e. at least six hours a day.

Watering is to a lesser extent affected by the weather but you do need to monitor whether there has been a lot of rain and whether you actually need to water that day, if the soil is moist and not dried out then you can miss a watering session. If you struggle to keep on top of your watering program then you may need to consider an automatic watering system.

* Top tip* – extremes of moisture and temperature are compounded by the use of containers that are too small; the minimum size pot that should be used is 12" diameter. The extra mass of compost slows the rate of temperature change and is less susceptible to drying out quickly.

Disease Control for Tomatoes

The main source of disease for tomatoes comes from the soil, so keeping lower trusses clear of the ground through pruning will help avoid contact with the ground.

Other than that you should have planted your tomatoes at least 18" (450mm) apart for good air circulation and when you water don't pour the water all over the plant, introduce the water to the base of the plant. This will help prevent the build up of moisture on the leaves which can cause mildew or bacterial infection.

Don't let the weeds around your tomato plants get a good hold; catch them early and clear them away. They will only compete with your plants for nutrients and may transfer problems to your plants if they are allowed to come into contact. Adding a mulch around the base of the plant will help keep weeds down.

Caring for tomatoes is often just a matter of using commonsense and keeping an eye out for problems. If you do find any diseased plants you may be able to cut out the diseased portions for disposal if you catch it early enough. Failing that you may have to remove the whole plant to protect the rest of the crop. Always remember to bag and bin diseased plants so that you don't contaminate compost or reintroduce the problem some other way.

If you need more information and help identifying what's wrong with your tomatoes, you can visit the Colorado State Extension page for recognising tomato problems

(www.ext.colostate.edu/pubs/garden/02949.html)

Points of Interest - Tomatoes, the wonder medicine

Take care of tomatoes and tomatoes will take care of you. In recent years the humble tomato, once regarded as a poisonous upstart, has had a very good press. Not only does it taste excellent when served alone and uncooked, apparently it confers even more benefits once cooked. The process encourages the release of certain chemicals that our bodies find useful in their perpetual campaign to ward off disease and ageing. Cancers and heart disease are singled out as maladies that can be fought off by a well-balanced diet rich in lycopene.

I must admit I eat tomatoes because I find them tasty. But having read a series of independent reports from scientists with no apparent axes to grind I may well step up my intake. I'm all for a long and active life and if tomatoes promote that . . . excellent. I shall just have to put up with more of them.

Lycopene, the red pigment that increases with ripeness, is a powerful antioxidant and helps prevent damage to arteries, cells and DNA. And wonder of wonders, unlike nutrients in most other fruits and vegetables, the act of cooking and processing tomatoes actually increases the efficacy rather than diminishes it. More goodness and well-being is released.

And the story gets better and better because if you then add a top quality oil to the tomato-containing dish before eating it, because lycopene is fat-soluble, the body will absorb the chemical more readily. Fantastic, not only do they taste great but they can also save your life!

Ripening Tomatoes

As with all vegetable growing, the one stage that every gardener awaits with eager anticipation is when the plants start to deliver ripe, ready to eat produce. This is when you can start to reap the rewards for all of your effort. Waiting for your tomatoes to ripen is no different to any other garden product.

The problem is tomatoes can sometimes be a little tricky and hang on the vine not looking at all like the lovely red tomatoes everyone aspires to.

There are a few good reasons for this, first of all the most obvious: not every tomato variety is red. In rare cases some are actually ripe and ready to eat when they are green. There are also varieties that are yellow, orange or even striped, so make sure you know which varieties you are growing so you know what to expect. Seems obvious but not everyone keeps a note of the type of tomato they are growing.

To an extent the type of tomato applies to the second reason some tomatoes can take longer to ripen, which is size. Clearly a small cherry-type tomato will ripen more quickly than a large beefsteak-type of tomato. The period to maturity and ripening can vary across tomato types by as much as 25 to 30 days, mostly size dependent.

That said, tomatoes of all varieties and types have to reach a mature stage, which is actually when they are still mostly green but maybe showing the beginning of turning red at the blossom end. Until they reach this mature state they will not ripen, even if you take them off the vine and try to induce ripening indoors for example. If you do try and induce ripening at some point you need to be sure the tomatoes have reached maturity before removing them from the plant.

What triggers ripening in tomatoes is ethylene gas which acts as a hormone to progress the ripening process. As they ripen they produce carotene and lycopene in the skin giving it the colour red. Tomatoes will normally ripen as long as the temperature is between 13C (55F) to 29C (85F); temperatures lower than this will produce bland, tasteless tomatoes and any higher than 29C (85F) and the production of carotene and lycopene will stall abruptly.

How to ripen tomatoes

If it is around the end of the growing season for your region with the colder nights coming in and perhaps a possibility of frost on the horizon, you will need to start thinking about how to ripen tomatoes that are still green before you lose them completely or have to commit them to the chutney option.

The two at the top, ready and ripe for the picking

One of the ways of ensuring that your tomatoes ripen is to continuously harvest your tomatoes as they become ready for picking. This releases energy to the tomatoes that are not quite ready and will encourage them to ripen.

Another general suggestion is that if you note that your night-time temperatures are dropping below 13C (55F) then there is little or no chance of any new blossoms becoming fruit, so pinch these out and direct the energy they would otherwise have taken to your fruit that still needs to ripen.

Another handy way of turning tomatoes that are in a greenhouse is to hang a bunch of bananas in the greenhouse with the tomatoes; the ripening bananas will give out the ethylene gas mentioned earlier which causes fruit to ripen. Bananas give it out in abundance, even after they have been picked. Why this works in a greenhouse is because it's an enclosed environment which allows the gas to concentrate in a confined space making it more effective.

Removing large fruit that are still green will give the smaller fruit more of a chance of getting the energy needed to ripen and if you select them correctly you may be able to place the removed tomatoes somewhere dark and dry to ripen them off; just check them every few days to make sure there is nothing going wrong or to see if they are ready to use.

If all else fails you can ripen tomatoes indoors but you have to get them off the vine before a heavy frost arrives; they can be protected up to a point by covering for light frosts but this is risky.

One method of ripening indoors is to take each tomato and wrap it in newspaper and place the wrapped tomatoes in a cardboard box up to two layers deep. Any more and the tomatoes on the bottom layer will tend to get bruised and damaged as they ripen, so stick to the two layer rule to be safe.

You can place a banana on the top to aid ripening if you want to; the tomatoes will produce their own ethylene gas as they ripen but a banana will add additional quantities of the much needed gas. Place the box in a dark dry place, avoid high humidity as this will tend to cause rotting of the fruit and check periodically for progress. Make sure any fruit that is showing signs of a problem is removed and disposed of.

Remember that temperature plays a part in the ripening process and the minimum temperature should be 13C (55F) for reasonable results; any lower and you will have tasteless, bland fruit. The ideal is between 18C (65F) to 21C (70F) for a speedy ripening period (two to three weeks) and tasty fruit.

Top Tips- Things that prevent tomatoes ripening: -

- insufficient sun light

- extreme temperatures cold or hot

- if the tomato is large in size, just needs more time

- erratic watering schedule, tomatoes like consistently damp soil that is neither dried out or saturated, although you can back off on the watering a little as they start to ripen

- not picking off the ripe fruit

- allowing too many blossoms, especially late in the season

- over fertilizing

Points of Interest - Tomatoes as weapons of mush destruction

For the past fifty-five years the world has shuddered at the thought of what atomic warfare might entail. World wars have thankfully been avoided in this time – often by the slimmest of margins – and as news and information ricochets around the world in seconds rather than days, weeks or months, perhaps we are better able to spot disturbances before they erupt into violence and madness. But somehow all this has escaped the notice of the inhabitants of the small town of Bunol, Valencia in Spain. My advice – avoid this town in late August each year unless you are prepared to experience a battle of such intensity that were it conducted with anything but tomatoes the results would be tragic in the extreme.

La Tomatina, the world's first and largest tomato-throwing fight, lasts exactly an hour each year and nowadays attracts over 40,000 young and not so young participants who like nothing better than to hurl rotten and soft tomatoes at each other until fatigue sets in. The photographs suggest a good time is had by all, and with each passing year more and more copycat events are taking place around the world. The date for your diary this year: check the website, link below. I'll see you there – in my dreams. Have a nice day!

(www.latomatina.es/en/)

Additional Resources for Tomato Growing

Home Grown Tomatoes (www.myhomegrowntomatoes.com/)

Royal Horticultural Society (www.rhs.org.uk/)

If you enjoyed reading this book and would like to share that enjoyment with others, then please take the time to visit the place where you made your purchase and write a review.

Reviews are a great way to spread the word about worthy authors and will help them be rewarded for their hard work.

Printed in Great Britain
by Amazon